The Drug Abuse Prevention Library

Drugs and Dieting

Many celebrities, such as Calista Flockhart, are very thin. This may encourage girls to pursue unhealthy and dangerous diets.

The Drug Abuse Prevention Library

Drugs and Dieting

Jeremy Roberts

The Rosen Publishing Group, Inc.
New York

Published in 2001 by The Rosen Publishing Group, Inc.
29 East 21st Street, New York, NY 10010

First Edition 2001

Library of Congress Cataloging-in-Publication Data

Roberts, Jeremy.
Drugs and dieting / by Jeremy Roberts.—1st ed.
p. cm. — (The drug abuse prevention library)
Includes bibliographical references.
ISBN 0-8239-3357-1
1. Appetite depressants—Health aspects—Juvenile literature. 2. Weight loss preparations—Health aspects—Juvenile literature. 3. Weight loss—Health aspects—Juvenile literature. [1. Appetite depressants. 2. Weight loss preparations. 3. Weight control. 4. Diet.]
I. Title. II. Series.
RM332.3 .R63 2001
615'.739—dc21

2001000018
Manufactured in the United States of America

Contents

Young women often feel pressured by society to be thin.

Introduction

Fourteen-year-old Amy never thought much about her body until the day she went to buy a bathing suit with her friend Chrissie. Chrissie walked directly to the rack full of tiny bikinis and when she tried one on, she looked like a movie star.

Amy felt a little sick. She trolled the racks for nearly an hour. Two-piece suits were definitely no good. Her body stuck out in all the wrong places. She thought the bikinis made her thighs look like elephant legs. Even the one-pieces were horrible. Desperate, she ended up buying a suit that looked more like a shopping bag.

Chrissie told Amy she was being silly, but what else would a friend say? When she got home, Amy picked up a magazine. Every girl and woman inside seemed to weigh half of what she weighed. They had trim waists, full breasts, and skinny thighs. She felt like a blob.

Amy decided she had to lose weight—and fast. Her boyfriend, Jed, also wanted to lose weight. He had been a varsity wrestler the year before. If he was going to do well he had to stay in the weight class he had been in last year, but he was already three pounds overweight.

Jed and Amy went to the library and checked out every book they could find on diets. By the time school started in the fall, they had tried four different diets. None seemed to work. Amy had gained five pounds. Jed had gained three. They decided they better look for another solution.

Television shows, magazines, and billboards shower us every day with images of buff bodies—thin is everywhere. The models posing in these photos are not just thin, but impossibly thin. Girls with no waists have large breasts. Guys have rippling abs and sleek shoulders.

We often compare ourselves to these images. It is impossible not to. We may realize that photographs are posed and in some cases altered. We may also realize that often models have undergone cosmetic surgery to enlarge their breasts or shrink their stomachs. Some models may starve themselves to stay thin. Yet we still feel inadequate.

So what do we do? Some of us laugh it off. Some of us shrug. And a lot of us try to force our bodies to look more like the bodies in those magazine pictures.

We diet, but never seem to lose weight. We exercise, but the scale still moves in the wrong direction. Meanwhile, the message comes through loud and clear: If you are not skinny, if you are not buff, you are worthless.

No one wants to feel unattractive or unworthy. Desperate to have their bodies conform to media ideals, some people start to look for other solutions. Sooner or later, some people even start using drugs that might help them lose weight. Unfortunately, this is just the moment when things can turn truly ugly.

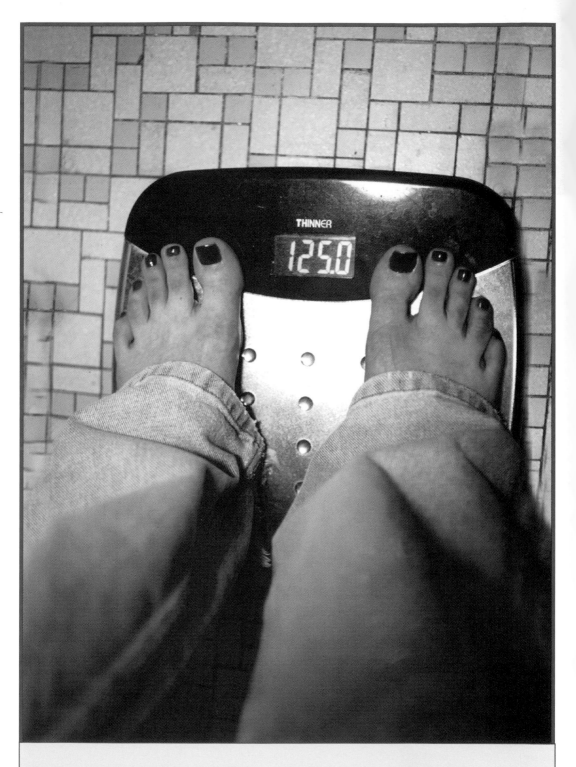

People come in different shapes, sizes, and weights.

How the Body Works

A my looked down at the scale in disgust. She had gained three pounds since she went on the latest diet! The jeans she had bought only three weeks ago no longer fit. And yet she had followed the diet instructions to the letter. It was time for desperate measures.

FOOD IS MORE THAN FUEL

The human body is often compared to an engine. Like an engine, it needs fuel to work. The body's fuel is food.

But bodies are more complicated than even the most advanced rocket engine. No two human bodies work in exactly the same way. And the nutritional needs of each body change over time.

For example, bodies that are growing rapidly, such as those belonging to older children and teenagers, need more fuel than adult bodies. Bodies that are very active tend to burn fuel more efficiently than less active bodies. Bodies starved for certain nutrients may crave those nutrients. They can even demand that outrageous amounts of food be consumed until those nutrients are found.

Food can also be used as more than just fuel. Sometimes people use food as a substitute for other things, like love. Sometimes people begin to view food as a poison to be avoided at all costs.

CALORIES AND CONTENT

Everyone needs a certain amount of food to survive. Doctors and nutritionists often describe how much food a healthy body requires in terms of calories. A calorie is a scientific measure of the energy in a piece of food. In fact, a calorie is the energy that is needed to raise the temperature of one gram of water by one degree centigrade.

As the calorie content of any food only represents the level of energy that food will provide, two foods with the same number of calories can have different weights, and certainly they have different tastes. They may also possess different minerals and other nutrients.

To lose weight, you should try to eat low-calorie meals as often as you can. A low-fat salad is healthier than a high-fat burger and fries.

The number of calories you need to eat every day or week depends on several factors: how much you currently weigh, how much your body is growing, and your level of physical activity. Doctors, nurses, dietitians, and other health professionals use formulas and charts to help people determine their dietary needs. But in general, most kids and young adults need to consume between 2,200 and 2,800 calories per day just to maintain their weight.

For most people, gaining or losing weight is a matter of counting calories. Eat more calories than your body needs and you will gain weight. Eat less and you will lose weight.

GENES

Genes influence your shape and size. The deoxyribonucleic acid (DNA) in genes forms the blueprint for your body. Some blueprints call for wide hips, others for narrow shoulders. Genes themselves may not make you fat or skinny. However, they may make it easier or harder for your weight to be within the range of what is considered normal, in terms of medical charts or societal expectations.

It is important to remember that calories and weight are only one dimension of health and nutrition. A person could eat an average number of calories every day and remain unhealthy if these calories are in the form of highly processed and sugary junk foods. Likewise, someone who is thin may not exercise enough. Many people also need extra vitamins and minerals that they do not receive from the foods they eat.

Dietitians, who study what we eat, say that people need to receive calories from many different types of foods. The United States Department of Agriculture (USDA) Food Guide Pyramid, published by the federal government, organizes foods into different groups. A balanced diet consisting of servings from each group is recommended. The number and size

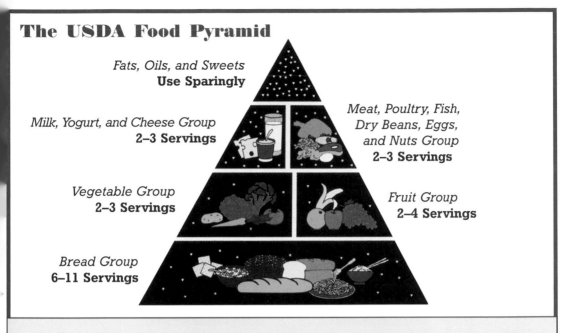

The USDA Food Pyramid

Fats, Oils, and Sweets
Use Sparingly

Milk, Yogurt, and Cheese Group
2–3 Servings

Meat, Poultry, Fish,
Dry Beans, Eggs,
and Nuts Group
2–3 Servings

Vegetable Group
2–3 Servings

Fruit Group
2–4 Servings

Bread Group
6–11 Servings

Following the food pyramid's guidelines for good nutrition is especially important if you are trying to lose weight.

of the servings a person requires depends on his or her individual needs. In general though, the pyramid recommends that people eat more grains, fruits, and vegetables and less meat and fewer fats, such as oil or butter.

TOO HEAVY?

Scientists say that many modern Americans eat more food than their bodies need. In fact, as many as 35 percent of adults, 14 percent of children, and 12 percent of teenagers are overweight. Medical professionals consider a small but growing percentage of young people obese. Obesity is a medical term for

Research has found that "couch potatoes" who are not physically active and watch a lot of television are more often obese than people who are active.

someone who is very overweight, usually someone who weighs 30 percent more than his or her medically recommended weight.

There are several reasons why so many Americans are overweight. One is simply the great bounty of food available to those Americans with the resources to buy it. Another is the fact that for many, daily life is simply less active than that of their ancestors.

Being very overweight can lead to long-term health problems. For example, being heavy may put too much strain on a person's heart and circulatory system. On the other hand, a body that is too thin may lack proper nutrients and this can stall growth. Over time, malnutrition can harm vital organs such as the heart or the brain. In severe cases, a person who is greatly underweight may risk a stroke or heart attack.

Until very recently, many people believed that being fat resulted from a lack of self-control. Certainly, love handles—a few extra pounds of fat around the upper hips—can result from eating too much and not exercising. Research, however, has shown that in other cases, weight gain is not that simple. In many cases, hormones in the body cause obesity. People gain weight due to genes and body chemistry, not because they lack willpower. Further, once someone adds a lot of extra weight to his or her body, body chemistry can make it more difficult to stop gaining, let alone lose weight.

Doctors, dietitians, and others who study nutrition believe that in the overwhelming majority of cases, simply exercising—sixty minutes a day for kids and young adults—and following a prudent diet will return a person to a healthy weight. Only in severe cases do they recommend the use of drugs.

Chapter

Diet Drugs

Amy was just plain disgusted. It seemed that no matter what she tried, she kept gaining weight. Two pounds one week, three the next—they just kept piling on. Jed, on the other hand, had lost nearly five pounds. He was weight training and looking pretty good. Amy worried he wouldn't want to be seen with her anymore. He was buff. She felt like a load.

Amy and Chrissie were hanging out after school. Amy stared at her superthin friend and finally blurted out, "What's your secret? How do you stay so thin?"

"These," said Chrissie. She opened her purse and showed Amy a little box of pills. "I stole them from my mom. Want some?"

Both prescription and nonprescription diet pills can have unhealthy side effects. In high doses, some can cause stroke, heart attack, and death.

AMPHETAMINES AS DIET PILLS

Decades ago, doctors routinely prescribed amphetamines as diet or "pep" pills. Amphetamines are a large family of drugs, each with its own special characteristics. Generally, amphetamines artificially stimulate the body. This stimulation convinces the brain and the rest of the body that it is not hungry. The pills seem to provide the body with extra energy or pep. Unfortunately, it took doctors many years to recognize that amphetamines have many unhealthy side effects. They are addictive and in high dosages can lead to stroke, heart attack, and death.

Amphetamines are now rarely, if ever, pre-scribed for weight loss. When used to treat a medical condition, they are highly controlled. Some people obtain these drugs illegally and attempt to use them to lose weight. But they are simply not worth the risk. Besides, they may not help. Studies have shown that in the long run, a careful diet combined with exer-cise helps people lose and keep off weight just as effectively as amphetamines.

Even so, many people continue to abuse amphetamines in the form of speed, "meth," and similar stimulants. Some people want to stay thin—regardless of the cost to their health. They do not realize that they are only making things worse.

NEW DRUGS

Scientists and researchers working for drug companies continually try to develop diet drugs to sell to consumers eager to find a quick and effective way to lose weight. The names of the chemicals and drugs are nearly as long as the diagrams of the molecules that form them. It may be years before any or all of these substances can be made into drugs.

The Federal Drug Administration (FDA) must test and approve drugs before they can be made available by prescription. Even then, it is likely that doctors will prescribe them only for severely overweight people. Since many of these drugs affect individual patients differently, doctors must decide which one is best for each patient. Like most other drugs, they may have side effects that doctors must monitor. Because many of these drugs are still somewhat new, some people question if they can be used safely.

Cholecystokinin (CCK)

One focus of current diet drug research is the role of peptides and hormones in the body. Peptides are combinations of amino acids that help govern many bodily functions. Among the body's peptides are those that assist or govern digestion and the hypothalamus. The hypothalamus is the area of the brain that regulates many bodily functions, such as breathing and heart rate. The hypothalamus regulates these functions through the use of hormones.

While peptides and hormones occur naturally in our bodies, chemists can create some artificially. Scientists interested in developing diet drugs study the relationship of peptides to eating and digestion. For example, when food enters the small intestine, a hormone called cholecystokinin, or CCK, is released

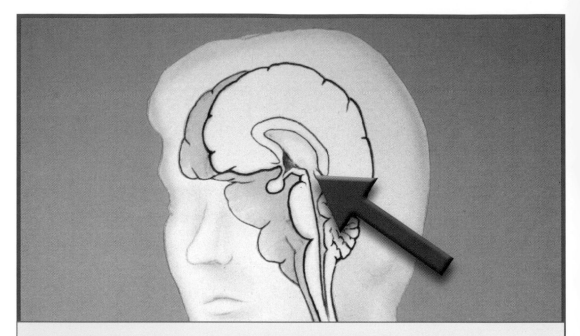

Diet drugs can change the way your hypothalamus (above) distributes hormones throughout your body.

into the bloodstream. One of the things this hormone does is to send commands that keep the stomach from emptying. This makes a person feel full, so he or she stops eating.

Some researchers believe that it may be possible to artificially introduce CCK into the body. By doing so, a person would feel artificially full and stop eating. However, because peptides are broken down routinely during the digestion process, CCK's effects are limited. Some studies performed on animals have shown that it may be possible to use CCK in a nose spray, thereby delaying its breakdown.

Amylin and glucagon are two of the many other peptides and hormones that scientists are investigating. The peptide amylin slows the emptying of the stomach. Glucagon is a hormone released by cells in the pancreas. When the hormone reaches the central nervous system, it is converted into a peptide that acts on the brain to suppress hunger.

Sympathomimetic Drugs

Among prescription drugs currently used to treat obesity are sympathomimetic diet drugs. Phentermine, mazindol, and diethylproprion are all sympathomimetic drugs. Basically, these drugs trick the body into thinking that it is not hungry. These drugs work by producing or preserving special chemicals in the brain called neurotransmitters.

These drugs stimulate the body to release neurotransmitters such as norepinephrine or serotonin. Neurotransmitters reduce the appetite by stimulating nerve cells and parts of the brain that control the appetite. In some cases, sympathomimetic drugs prevent cells from absorbing norepinephrine, enabling the norepinephrine to continue stimulating appetite control.

All sympathomimetic drugs are controlled substances and must be prescribed by a doctor. Because they can be abused, doctors prescribe them very rarely. Most are only

Some prescription diet drugs influence the chemicals in your brain so that your body thinks it is not hungry.

used for very short periods of time, usually no more than three months. They should always be used in conjunction with a careful diet and exercise plan.

Orlistat

Another new drug used to help obese people lose weight is orlistat. Its trade name is Xenical. Unlike sympathomimetic diet drugs that aim to control appetite, orlistat blocks the absorption of fat. There is still some debate about the safety and effectiveness of the drug, but some doctors believe it can help reduce weight when used in conjunction with a proper diet plan. In some people, the drug has caused mild side effects such as gas pains and changes in bowel movements.

Fen-Phen

The diet drug fen-phen is actually a combination of two drugs: phentermine and fenfluramine. Phentermine speeds up the body's metabolism. It is a prescription sympathomimetic drug. It makes the body increase its production of neurotransmitters. Phentermine works in the same way as some amphetamines, but without as many side effects.

Fenfluramine is another diet drug. It reduces hunger by telling the body to create serotonin, an important body chemical. In effect, it tells the brain that the body is already full.

Doctors began using the two drugs separately to treat obese people several years ago. While the drugs helped somewhat, they did not produce dramatic results. Then one day a doctor wondered if combining them might make a more effective diet drug. As the drugs attacked the problem of overeating in different ways, the doctor realized that, together, they might make a powerful team.

Soon thereafter, a major study revealed that patients using the new drug combination lost nearly three times as much weight as

A lawyer gestures toward a heart diagram while arguing the fen-phen case. American Home Products had to pay $4.8 billion to settle claims that its diet drug caused life-threatening heart valve problems in users.

those who were not using the drugs at all. The combination became known as fen-phen.

Initially, fen-phen was considered a wonder drug. Many people took it and lost a considerable amount of weight. Then, in 1997, doctors discovered a severe side effect. In some cases, people using fen-phen developed potentially fatal heart valve damage on the left side of their hearts. Doctors also discovered that patients using fenfluramine exclusively also developed this heart problem. The drug's manufacturer, American Home Products, took fenafluramine and dexfenfluramine, a related drug, off the market. American Home Products now faces many lawsuits. (Phentermine, when used without fenfluramine, is not known to have similar side effects. Nonetheless, its use is still highly controlled.)

While other drugs that work in similar ways may not have these side effects, the fen-phen scare shows how difficult it is to find a diet drug that is safe and effective. It also reminded doctors and other experts that except in special cases, people who want to lose weight should simply focus on maintaining a balanced diet and a program of exercise.

OTHER PRESCRIPTION DRUGS

Drugs that are not diet drugs can also affect an individual's metabolism or the way the body processes and regulates energy. In this way, these drugs also affect weight. Birth control pills (because they often contain estrogen), for example, can cause women's bodies to retain water. The water retained becomes added weight.

People with thyroid problems sometimes take a drug called liothyronine, or T3. In some cases, this drug can cause weight loss. In most cases, when used properly, the side effects of this drug are minimal. Anyone experiencing side effects should consult a doctor.

OVER-THE-COUNTER MEDICATIONS

Some drugs used for appetite control are considered safe. Adults do not need a special prescription to buy them. Until recently, the most common diet drug in America was probably phenylprepanolamine, or PPA. While it is similar to an amphetamine, initially the drug was thought to be much safer. It was available over the counter. Popular diet drugs such as Acutrim and Dexatrim contained PPA. PPA was also an ingredient in some cold medications.

In 2000, scientists found that PPA might cause strokes in some young people. Soon after this information was released, companies that made products that contained PPA began to take them off the market. The FDA, which regulates drugs, decided after examining the study that no drugs containing PPA should remain on the market.

Some people abuse other over-the-counter medications in an attempt to quickly lose weight. Some dieters, desperate to suppress their appetites, turn to caffeine pills. They take them for energy and as a substitute for food.

People sometimes abuse laxatives and diuretics. Rather than suppressing their appetite, people ingest these drugs after eating in an attempt to rid the body of food at a highly increased rate. Laxatives force the digestive system to dispose of food before it is properly processed. Abusing laxatives can lead to many problems, including damage to the colon and the rest of the digestive system.

Diuretics are over-the-counter medications that force the body to eliminate water and liquid wastes. The use of diuretics also depletes the body of important substances such as potassium and electrolytes that help nerve cells to communicate and muscles to function. Also, without electrolytes, cells throughout the body cannot maintain their proper fluid balance.

Alcohol and Nicotine

Substances such as alcohol and nicotine can also have an effect on weight. Alcohol sometimes dampens the appetite by replacing good calories from food with "empty" calories from alcohol. It tricks the body into thinking it has eaten enough.

Smoking cigarettes may speed up your metabolism. On the other hand, some studies have shown that nicotine may cause the body to store more fat. It may also

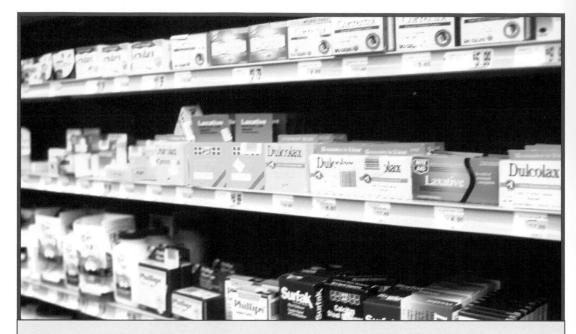

There are hundreds of diet drugs and supplements available. As with any other medications, these should be taken with care.

interfere with the body's normal use of calories and nutrients.

DRUGS AND WEIGHT CONTROL

Drugs can play a role in weight control. Doctors and pharmacists believe they may help many obese people return to safer, healthier weight levels. But they are only one part of a weight-reduction plan. Like any drug, diet medications must be taken carefully and only after receiving a doctor's advice.

Amy was tempted by the pills. She looked at the box longingly. But she had seen a program on television a few nights ago about a girl who had accidentally overdosed on prescription drugs. Even though this wasn't the same thing, she felt her stomach start to turn.

"No, thanks," she said.

"Up to you," said Chrissie.

"Maybe I should talk to a doctor about taking something," said Amy.

"What do doctors know?" Chrissie laughed. "My brother is studying to be a doctor and you know what a geek he is."

Still, Amy didn't touch the pills.

Herbs and Supplements

*J*ed was losing weight, but it was a real struggle. Once the holidays rolled around, he would never be able to maintain his wrestling weight without help.

One night, he was fooling around on the Internet and decided to use a search engine to look for help. Two clicks later, he was reading about miracle pills used for centuries in China. All sorts of people used them—bodybuilders, cops, a race car driver. Before and after pictures tried to show that they really were a miracle.

If Jed had a credit card, he would have ordered a bottle. In fact, Jed was tempted to sneak into his mom's pocketbook and borrow hers.

BEYOND DIET PILLS

Diet pills are not the only substances that promise quick weight loss. We do not usually think of herbs and vitamin and mineral supplements as drugs. Nevertheless, some can have the same effects.

Because herbs, vitamins, and minerals are not sold as drugs, they are not tested in the same way. Herbs may seem particularly safe because they are advertised as "natural" products. They are often found in supermarkets and health food stores as well as drug stores. But they can still pose risks.

The amount of an herb actually contained in a product can vary greatly from brand to brand. In some cases, herbs are sold as a tea or in drinks. The amount of an active ingredient contained in a pill can differ from manufacturer to manufacturer.

These substances are not tested or regulated by the FDA, and there are often no accepted standard doses. Production methods and purity can also differ from brand to brand. Those who sell herbs can make claims that are not subject to the same rules drug manufacturers must follow. In some cases, these claims are exaggerations or simply lies.

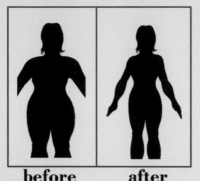

Lose weight now!!

"I lost 40 lbs. in JUST 6 WEEKS!
I was able to eat ANYTHING
that I wanted!
I am so much happier with
my NEW body"
-Jane Doe, USA

Super Drug!

100% NATURAL HERBS

before   after

Many companies promise amazing results from their diet products. Just remember: If a claim sounds too good to be true, it's probably false.

EPHEDRA

One of the most popular herbs sold for weight loss today is ephedra. It is also known as Ma huang, Chinese ephedra, epitonin, and ephedrine. It comes from a shrub grown in Asia. Sometimes ephedrine is combined with caffeine to increase its effectiveness.

The active ingredient in the ephedra plant is ephedrine. It is a stimulant. In fact, a human-made form of ephedrine can be found in medications for bronchitis, allergies, and colds. It decreases appetite and speeds up the body's metabolism, helping to burn calories. Some manufacturers also claim that unidentified ingredients that occur in the plant increase ephedrine's effect.

Unfortunately, ephedrine can have side effects, such as heart attacks, seizures, and nerve damage. The risk of experiencing these side effects increases when ephedrine is used improperly. Less severe side effects include high blood pressure and insomnia. In 1999, the FDA received 900 reports from doctors and individuals of side effects from ephedrine. The scope of these effects varied, but health reports say that at least thirty cases resulted in death.

Manufacturers who sell the herb say that it is safe when used according to the directions on the label. They point out that people have used the herb for centuries in Asia and claim that they follow precise standards when making ephedrine. Yet, some states have banned or are considering banning the sale of ephedrine products to teenagers.

OTHER HERBS

A number of other herbs and plant products are sold as diet aids. It is difficult to verify their effectiveness. For instance, gum guggul is an extract of a plant grown in India known as guggul. Some studies have shown that the substance may help lower levels of harmful cholesterol in the body. But there have not been many Western studies of the substance. Side effects include diarrhea, skin rashes, and restlessness.

People who believe guggul can help with weight loss often point out that it is included in the ancient Indian healing art known as Ayurveda. Ayurveda views disease as the result of an imbalance in the forces that influence health. These forces can be changed in a number of ways, including the use of herbal remedies. Other weight-loss substances used in Ayurveda include amla or Indian gooseberry, behada or bahira, and harada or hairtaki. All are derived from plants. Most researchers in the West have yet to closely study these substances.

VITAMINS AND MINERALS

Vitamins are organic substances that are essential to all animals, including humans. They serve as coenzymes and as precursors to enzymes. In this way, they enable vital organic functions in the body's cells and metabolic processes. Minerals also play a crucial role in some of these processes.

Both vitamins and essential minerals are an important part of a balanced diet. A

You can ingest vitamins by eating healthy foods or by taking supplements.

well-balanced and varied diet should provide most, if not all, necessary vitamins. In many cases, doctors recommend that their patients take specific vitamins and multivitamins to ensure that all of their bodily needs are met.

In the past few years, some minerals and vitamins have been touted for weight control. Among the most popular is chromium picolinate. It may or may not reduce weight by increasing the body's sensitivity to insulin, a hormone secreted by cells in the pancreas that plays an essential role in metabolizing carbohydrates. Studies on chromium picolinate are still being performed. While it is an important ingredient in a healthy diet, it is not a good

Natural fiber helps maintain proper health. It makes your stomach feel full and pushes fatty foods through your digestive system and out of your body.

substitute for a balanced diet. By itself, it seems unlikely to help one lose weight.

Scientists are still trying to learn more about vitamins and minerals. But as they do, it is good to remember the old adage: Everything in moderation. The federal government publishes recommended dosages of many vitamins and minerals. Taking a bit more than the recommended dose in many cases will do no harm, but it probably will not help. Taking too much can prove toxic.

FIBER SUPPLEMENTS

If you feel full, you will probably stop eating. That is one of the ideas behind the use of fiber supplements to limit weight gain. Dietary fiber can be found in many foods, such as cereal, oatmeal, and fruits. It helps the digestive tract function properly. Eating proper amounts of fiber can prevent constipation and other stomach ailments. Dietary fiber can also help the body absorb important nutrients. Some studies have shown that it may help reduce the risk of cancer and high cholesterol.

Fiber can be isolated, separated from foods, and taken separately in supplement form. Some fiber supplements are sold as weight-loss aids. Because in its natural form fiber is bulky, it takes up a lot of space in the digestive tract and makes a person feel full. Scientists have some doubts about the effectiveness of fiber in supplement form, and most recommend that people get their fiber naturally, from food. In supplement form, fiber might even prove harmful. In fact, some fiber supplements, like pectin, may actually increase the risk of cancer.

STEROID-LIKE SUBSTANCES

Some substances promise to increase weight. These promises can seem tempting, especially for those who want bigger bodies. Steroids and so-called pre-steroid substances are often sold to bodybuilders and other athletes.

Many do produce short-term results and help build muscles quickly. But in the long term, these substances can have many dangerous effects. Cancer and heart attack are among the dangers doctors cite when warning people to stay away from such supplements.

FOOD ADDITIVES AND SUBSTITUTES

What about fake sugar and pretend fat? Do they really help you lose weight? Since they contain fewer calories than the real thing, sugar and fat substitutes can help a person lose weight—in theory. Interestingly, studies show that most people make up for the saved calories by eating more. It may be that the body realizes it is being cheated by the substitutes and pushes for more food. Or it may be that people eating diet substances simply lose track of how much they are eating.

Anyone interested in losing—or gaining—weight should read food labels carefully. Pay attention to calories, not words like "diet" or "fat free." Food that is "fat free" may still be high in calories.

CONSULT A PROFESSIONAL

Many people have become interested in alternative medicine and the relationship between nutrition and health. They are eating healthy food and adding vitamins and minerals to their diets. Overall, this is a good trend. People are becoming more focused on their well-being. However, it is easy to become confused about the value of different substances. Consult a nutritionist or doctor before buying any herbs or supplements to lose weight.

Jed printed out the information on the miracle drug. He planned on talking to his dad about it. His father came to many of his wrestling meets and had always supported his efforts to improve as an athlete.

But before he could ask his father to buy the miracle herb, Jed happened to run into the wrestling coach at school.

"You're trying out for the team, right?" the coach asked in the cafeteria.

"Uh-huh," said Jed.

"Well, make sure you clean your plate," said the coach, pointing at his lunch. "I was hoping you would move up two weight classes this year. Johnson over at Deluge High graduated. I think you'll have a chance at the state championship in that weight class, if you fill out like you should."

Disorders

O ne morning, Chrissie was acting
a little strange. She giggled a
lot and seemed unable to finish
her sentences. Still, Amy didn't think
anything was seriously wrong until they
left homeroom. They were halfway
down the hall to their lockers when
Chrissie suddenly turned to her.

"I d-d-don't fee-eel . . . " Chrissie stut-
tered. Then her eyes rolled back in her
head. The next thing Amy knew,
Chrissie was on the floor. When Amy
knelt down by Chrissie's side, Chrissie
was shaking and as cold as ice.

ANOREXIA AND BULIMIA

Teenagers often rank body image and
weight among their most important concerns.
Is it any wonder? The media constantly bom-
bards us with images of an ideal body type,

one that most of us can only attain through unhealthy measures.

Experts say that teens are especially vulnerable to eating disorders. Eating disorders affect both men and women. The National Medical Society has estimated that as many as 1 percent of all teenage and young women in the United States are anorexic. Another 3 percent suffer from bulimia.

These disorders involve both a person's mind and his or her body. Someone who is anorexic believes that he or she weighs too much. In order to lose weight, anorexics begin to starve themselves. Anorexics often use drugs as part of their weight-loss strategy. With his or her body already depleted from improper nutrition, the use of drugs can put a person who is anorexic in grave danger.

Anorexia may begin strictly in the mind. For instance, a girl might believe that she has to lose weight to be attractive. At first, the ailment may be only in her head: She thinks she is fat, even though her weight is normal. Soon enough, a lack of food begins to affect her body. She is starving herself to death. This behavior endangers the heart and blood vessels. The kidneys and liver lack the proper nutrients to function normally. Bones can become brittle from lack

Athletes such as Derek Jeter can be good role models. But obsessing over obtaining a particular body type can lead to distortions in self-image and serious health problems.

of calcium. The body begins to literally eat itself to keep going.

An anorexic refuses to eat even when he or she is already very thin. The person continues to believe that he or she is fat. A binge-eating/purging anorexic binges by eating a great deal of food. He or she then purges himself or herself of it. Sometimes anorexics do this by vomiting. They may also take laxatives or other drugs that prevent the food from being properly digested.

In many respects, bulimia nervosa is similar to anorexia. A person who is bulimic has many episodes of binge eating that are usually followed by unusual efforts to lose the food consumed. A person who is bulimic also has a distorted body image. But because the weight loss may not be as severe as that experienced by an anorexic, it is often difficult to notice when someone is suffering from bulimia.

In extreme cases, people with anorexia or bulimia may require hospitalization. They can even die. Fortunately, professionals who deal with young people recognize these dangers. Besides doctors and nurses, many psychologists and counselors are trained to help young people deal with anorexia and other eating disorders. When an eating disorder is diagnosed early, a full recovery is usually possible.

HYPOTHYROIDISM

Some weight problems are not due to overeating or lack of exercise. People who have hypothyroidism, for example, have a problem with their thyroid gland. The thyroid regulates a person's metabolism. In some ways, it is like an internal thermostat. By releasing the thyroid hormone, the thyroid stimulates growth, speeds up the effect of insulin in the body, and helps the body respond to different hormones.

When the thyroid does not produce enough thyroid hormone, doctors say it is underactive. They call this condition hypothyroidism. A person with hypothyroidism gains weight because the rate at which his or her body normally functions slows down. There can be other side effects as well, such as constipation and a general feeling of depression or exhaustion.

Sometimes, the effects of hypothyroidism can be hard to notice. Fortunately, a simple blood test can measure the level of thyroid hormone in the bloodstream. If it is too low, a doctor can prescribe an artificial replacement.

Any doctor can test for this ailment. But there are special doctors who deal with this problem. They are called endocrinologists because the thyroid is part of the endocrine system. They are experts regarding the body's endocrine glands, including the pancreas, pituitary and adrenal glands, and the thyroid.

PROFESSIONAL HELP

Weight loss and weight gain can be signs of other disorders. In some instances, they are early warning signs of more serious problems. That is why it is important to discuss sudden weight shifts with your doctor or nurse.

Of course, many people are shy about their bodies. They may feel ashamed of a weight gain or loss. Sometimes parents and friends send mixed messages as well. They may not take a boy who is worried about being fat seriously. Or they may harshly criticize a girl who has put on a few extra pounds.

It is understandable to feel nervous about discussing weight or body image, but it is important to take control of your body and your health. Professionals such as nutritionists, nurses, and doctors can guide and assist you. In most cases, drugs do little to reduce weight and can cause dangerous side effects. In the few cases where drugs are appropriate, health professionals can help advise you on how to use them properly.

Amy found Jed during the study hall period they shared. She told him everything that had happened to Chrissie. "The school psychologist thinks she was using these pills to keep her weight down," Amy said. "I guess the pills had been prescribed for her mother. I know he's right, because she showed them to me once."

"Did you tell him?" asked Jed.

"I had to," said Amy. "Chrissie could have died. The psychologist says she is almost 10 percent underweight. She might even be anorexic."

"Yeah. You had to," agreed Jed.

"They're not even diet pills. They are like, for a thyroid condition or something," said Amy.

"Is she going to be okay?"

Amy shrugged. She could feel herself starting to cry. She hated to see her friends in trouble.

A Solid Plan

*S*ince she had to see her doctor for a regular checkup anyway, Amy decided to discuss her weight concerns with the doctor. Amy stammered at first. Then the words just gushed out. "I feel like a fat pimple!" she exclaimed.

To Amy's surprise, the doctor didn't laugh. Instead, she took out a file that contained information about Amy's height and weight ever since she was an infant. The doctor showed Amy that her growth had been steady. Then she compared Amy's current height and weight to another chart. Amy nearly fell over when she saw that she was normal.

"That doesn't mean that you can't improve your health," said the doctor. She recommended that Amy talk to a dietitian. She also gave Amy a pamphlet that outlined an exercise program.

The most surprising thing was Amy's mom's reaction. "I really should be getting more exercise," her mom confessed. "Maybe we could do some of this together."

BALANCED NUTRITION

Calorie needs differ from person to person, depending on many factors. These factors may include a person's age, height, or level of physical activity. In general, however, experts say that calorie intake should include a variety of foods.

Generally, you should try to eat several servings of fruits and vegetables a day. Such servings might include an apple or a helping of string beans or a glass of orange juice. Eating natural grains instead of processed food is another good way to maintain nutrition and remain at an ideal weight. While red meat is high in protein, it contains large amounts of harmful, saturated fat. Fish and poultry are important sources of protein that have less harmful fat. Some vegetable sources of protein, like beans and soy products, contain no harmful saturated fat at all. In general, it is best to limit fat intake to between 20 and 30 percent of your diet.

Eating a healthy, well-balanced diet can help you lose weight or maintain your weight without endangering your health.

Specific plans can be drawn up with the help of a dietitian or a nutritionist. Some nurses are also trained in this area. Many books are available on nutrition and health; a few are mentioned in the Where to Go for Help section at the back of this book. The federal government also offers publications and Web sites with basic nutrition information. It is best to avoid fad diets, so often promoted in the latest books and magazines and on television shows. Experts say old-fashioned variety and simple nutritious foods are the best way to maintain a healthy diet.

PROPER EXERCISE

Our bodies thrive when we lead physically active lives. With the introduction of labor-saving devices such as cars and computers into modern daily life, opportunities for physical activity at work or at home have decreased. Many health experts say that Americans of all ages need to exercise more. Organized programs of exercise like running, biking, aerobics, and weight training can become an important part of a healthy life. Most school sports coaches can recommend a workout regimen. Some doctors and nurses, especially those that practice sports medicine, can also help. They can develop diet and nutrition plans that enhance performance in specific sports.

Formal exercise programs are not the only way to increase physical activity. Simply doing active things that are fun will keep your body in shape and your weight at a healthy level. In-line skating, for example, is considered great exercise. Biking is just as good. Just routinely walking instead of taking a car everywhere can positively impact your health. Experts recommend that kids and teenagers get at least sixty minutes of physical activity every day. This can include anything from playing tag to running for the school bus.

Exercising regularly is the best way to reach and maintain your normal weight and maintain good health.

When it comes to exercise, it is important to remember not to overdo it, especially at first. A body that is not used to intense exercise can be easily injured. It is best to take a long-term approach. Don't look for results in an hour or a day. Quick fixes like drugs, supplements, and herbs that promise to multiply the effects of exercise are often misleading. These promises are almost always too good to be true.

ARE YOU OVERWEIGHT?

Media images often influence our idea of the perfect body. Unfortunately, the media rarely shows a wide variety of human body types. The images of health and success we see are usually limited to a very narrow range of possibilities. Our genes, however, are varied. Our bodies should be, too. If you believe that you are overweight, you should talk to your family doctor or the school nurse about it.

WHAT TO DO

Most experts suggest diet plans that result in a small and gradual reduction of daily calories for a person who is truly overweight and has no other medical problems. That means that the person will eat a few hundred calories less than what his or her body requires to maintain his or her existing weight. When combined with proper exercise, such a diet will allow the body to burn some of its stored fat.

In theory, a person on such a diet will lose between a half-pound and two pounds a week. Some weeks, the person will lose more, some weeks less. At times, his or her weight may actually increase. But sticking to the diet over a long period of time will produce lasting results.

A slow but steady weight loss is easier on the body than a huge loss in a short period of time. It is also easier to maintain. In fact, rapid weight loss is often followed by rapid weight gain. This can be just as harmful to one's health as obesity.

People who are underweight should follow basically the same procedure. Exercise should be an important part of their program as well. They should also eat a well-rounded diet with many nutrients, adding calories in a balanced manner.

Both Amy and Jed continued to gain weight during the school year. But in both cases, their gains were normal. Jed combined his wrestling exercise with some weight training and yoga for increased flexibility. He even made it to the state wrestling championships. He finished eighth: not bad for a junior.

With the help of her doctor, Amy changed her diet to include more fruits and vegetables. She started doing some aerobics exercises with her mom, but realized they weren't for her. Then she discovered rock climbing. Now she spends nearly every weekend scaling the mountains nearby. She even got Jed hooked—though he's not nearly as good as she is.

Chrissie recovered from her fainting spell. With the help of a doctor and a psychologist, she regained her health.

Glossary

amphetamines   A family of drugs that speed up the body's activities. Sometimes called "pep pills" or "uppers."

anabolic steroids   Steroids that affect the body's growth. Related to testosterone, anabolic steroids have dangerous side effects. While they can cause temporary weight and muscle gains, experts say the harm they can cause far outweighs the benefits.

anorexia nervosa   An eating disorder that causes a person to lose a lot of weight yet still believe that he or she is fat. Medically, a person who is anorexic is less than 85 percent of his or her expected weight.

appetite   The desire for food.

calorie   A measure of energy in food. To be exact, a calorie is the energy that is needed to raise one gram of water one degree centigrade.

diet   What a person eats. Also refers to a specific plan to lose or gain weight.

diet drug   A special substance used to help people lose weight. Doctors prescribe diet drugs only in special circumstances, usually if someone is very overweight or obese.

dietitian   Someone who has studied nutrition and diet.

eating disorder   A general term used by doctors and other health professionals to describe a condition, such as anorexia, in which abnormal eating patterns severely affect a person's health.

food pyramid   A chart prepared by the federal government showing the recommended daily helpings of food in a healthy diet.

herb   Any plant material used for medicinal purposes.

hormone   A product of certain cells in the body that controls processes in other cells. Hormones are believed to play an important role in the body's metabolism and may influence appetite.

ideal weight   A range of weight thought to be appropriate for most people. This is usually determined according to age, height, and body frame. Ideal weight can vary from person to person.

metabolism The processes the body uses
to grow and maintain life. Metabolism uses
the body's energy and nutrients, some of
which are obtained from food.

nutrients Substances that the body
needs to survive. These include
proteins, fats, carbohydrates, vitamins,
and essential minerals.

nutritionist Someone who has
studied nutrition.

obesity A medical term describing the
condition of being severely overweight.

performance enhancers General term
for a wide range of substances that sup-
posedly improve athletic performance.

supplements Substances such as vitamins
that are used to improve overall health.

steroids Substances used for a variety of
purposes by the body. When used
without proper medical supervision, manufactured or artificial steroids can have
serious and dangerous side effects.

sympathomimetic diet drugs Drugs that
reduce hunger by acting on special
chemicals in the body called neurotransmitters. All are prescription drugs and
are generally used for short periods.

Where to Go for Help

IN THE UNITED STATES

American Anorexia Bulimia Association
165 West 46th Street, Suite 1108
New York, NY 10036
(212) 575-6200
Web site: http://www.aabainc.org

American Council for Drug Education
164 West 74th Street
New York, NY 10023
(800) 488-DRUG (3784)
Web site: http://www.acde.org

American Dietetic Association
216 West Jackson Boulevard
Chicago, IL 60606-6995
(312) 899-0040
(800) 366-1655
Web site: http://www.eatright.org

National Clearinghouse for Alcohol
    and Drug Information
P.O. Box 2345
Rockville, MD 20847-2345
(800) 729-6686
Web site: http://www.health.org

HOTLINES

National Institute on Drug Abuse
    Referral Hotline
(800) 662-HELP (4357)
All calls are confidential.

Vegetarian Resource Group
P.O. Box 1463, Dept. IN
Baltimore, MD 21203
(410) 366-8343
Web site: http://www.vrg.org/nutrition/
    teennutrition.htm

IN CANADA

Canadian Centre on Substance Abuse
75 Albert Street, Suite 300
Ottawa, ON K1P 5E7
(613) 235-4048
Web site: http://www.ccsa.ca

Canadian Healthcare Association
17 York Street
Ottawa, ON K1N 9J6
(613) 241-8005
Web site: http://www.canadian-healthcare.org

Canadian Society for Exercise Physiology
185 Somerset Street West, Suite 202
Ottawa, ON K2P 0J2
(613) 234-3755
(877) 651-3755
Web site: http://www.csep.ca

Dietitians of Canada
480 University Avenue, Suite 604
Toronto, ON M5G 1V2
(416) 596-0857
Web site: http://www.dietitians.ca

WEB SITES

Health Canada Online
http://www.hc-sc.gc.ca/english

USDA Food and Nutrition Information Center
http://www.nal.usda.gov/fnic

For Further Reading

Barrett, Cece. *The Dangers of Diet Drugs and Other Weight-Loss Products.* New York: The Rosen Publishing Group, Inc., 1999.

Brody, Jane. *Jane Brody's Nutrition Book*, rev. ed. New York: Bantam Books, 1987.

Clayton, Lawrence. *Diet Pill Drug Dangers.* Springfield, NJ: Enslow, 1999.

Goldberg, Burton. *Weight Loss: An Alternative Medicine Definitive Guide.* Tiburon, CA: Alternative Medicine.Com Books, 2000.

Herbert, Victor, and Genell J. Subak-Sharpe, eds. *The Mount Sinai School of Medicine Complete Book of Nutrition.* New York: St. Martin's Press, 1990.

Salter, Charles A. *The Nutrition-Fitness Link: How Diet Can Help Your Body and Mind.* Brookfield, CT: Millbrook Press, 1993.

Samz, Jane. *Drugs and Diet.* New York: Chelsea House, 1988.

Index

ABOUT THE AUTHOR

Jeremy Roberts is the author of a number of books for young people, including *The Real Deal: A Guy's Guide to Being a Guy*, published by the Rosen Publishing Group.

PHOTO CREDITS

Cover by Cindy Reiman; p. 2 © Robert Bertoia/The Everett Collection; pp. 6, 10, 15, 16, 19, 24, 30 by Sarah Kuntsler; pp. 13, 37, 38, 51 by Cindy Reiman; p. 22 © Custom Medical; p. 26 © AP/Worldwide; p. 34 by Thomas Forget; p. 44 © Corbis; p. 53 © The Image Bank.